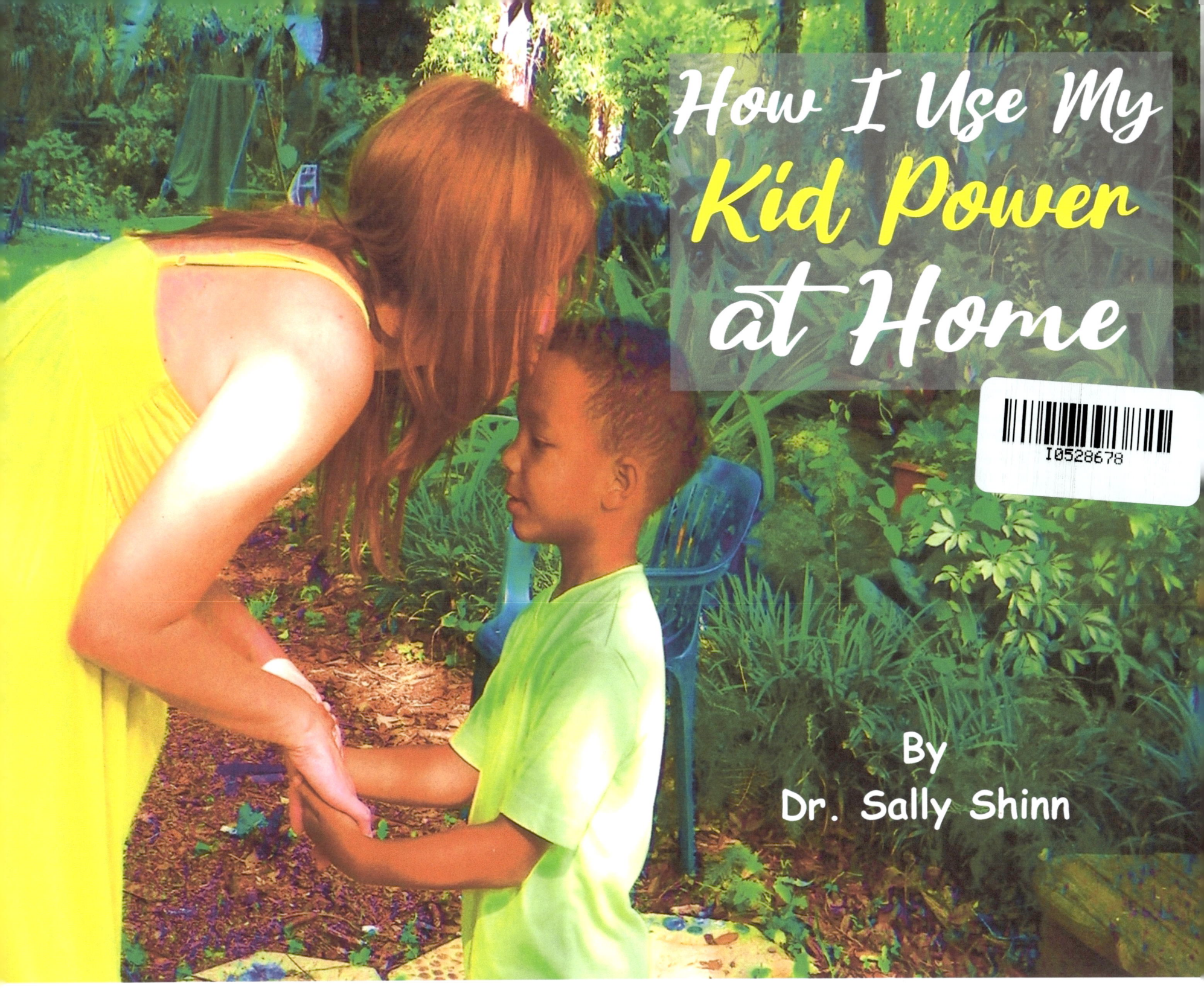

How I Use My Kid Power at Home

By

Dr. Sally Shinn

I0528678

Published in the United States of America

ISBN 978-1-962569-80-4 (SC)
ISBN 978-1-962569-78-1 (HC)
ISBN 978-1-962569-79-8 (Ebook)

Sally Shinn Publishing
222 West 6th Street
Suite 400, San Pedro, CA, 90731
sallyshinn0103@gmail.com

Order Information and Rights Permission:

Quantity sales. Special discounts might be available on quantity purchases by corporations, associations, and others. For details, contact the publisher at the address above.

For Book Rights Adaptation and other Rights Permission.
Call us at toll-free 1-888-945-8513 or send us an email at admin@stellarliterary.com.

This book is dedicated to working moms and to little children who are ready to contribute to their families in many ways.

My Momma has to work long hours to help our family. Sometimes she doesn't get done with her job until I am fast asleep at night.

2

My mom takes good care of me.

3

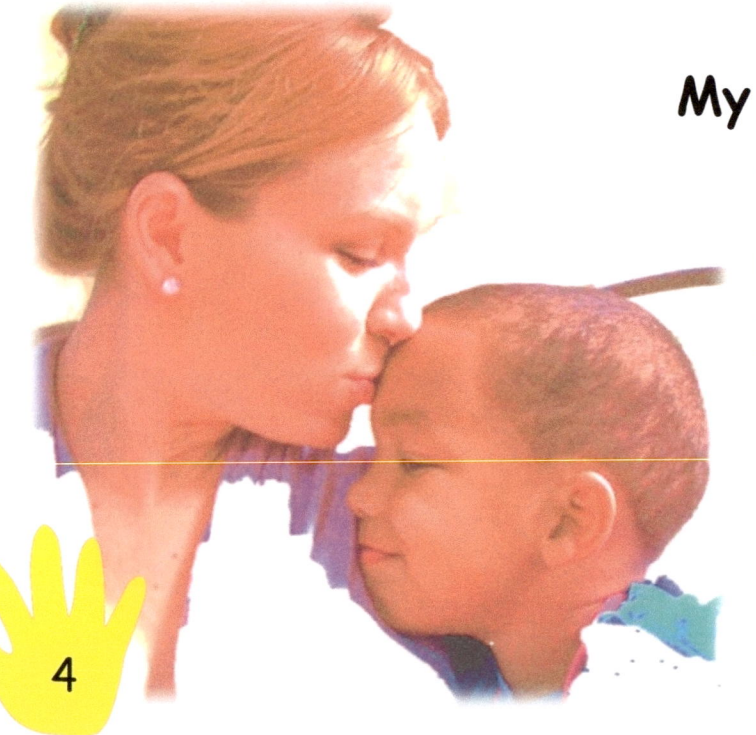

My Momma shows me
that she loves me
in so many ways.
I sure love her!

4

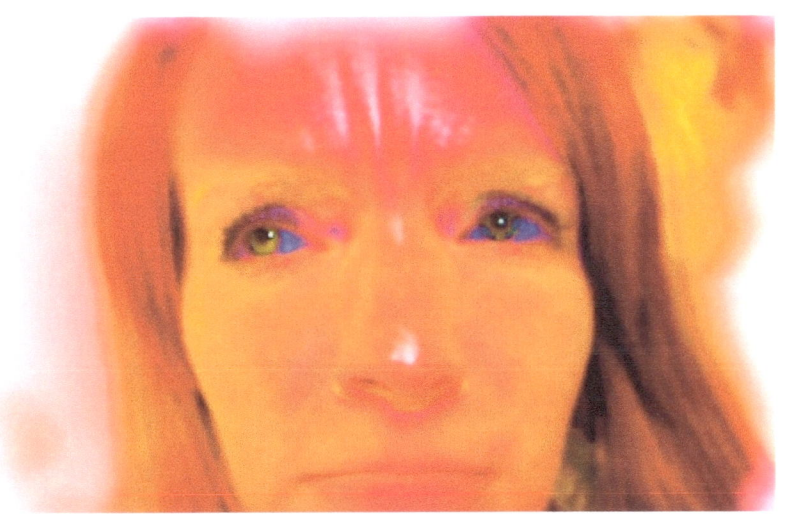

When Momma SMILES,
it's great to see... But a messy
house takes that smile away!

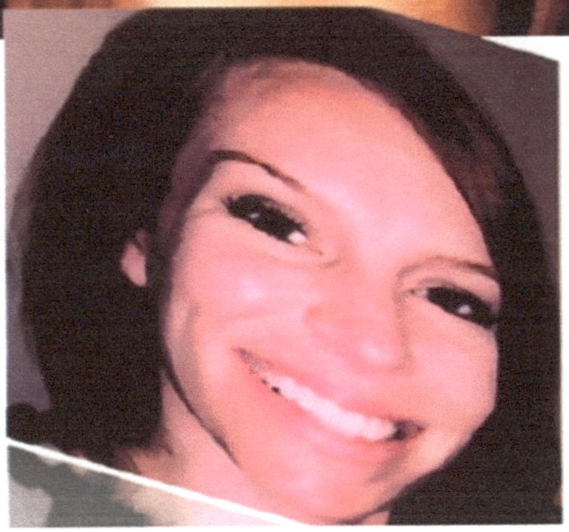

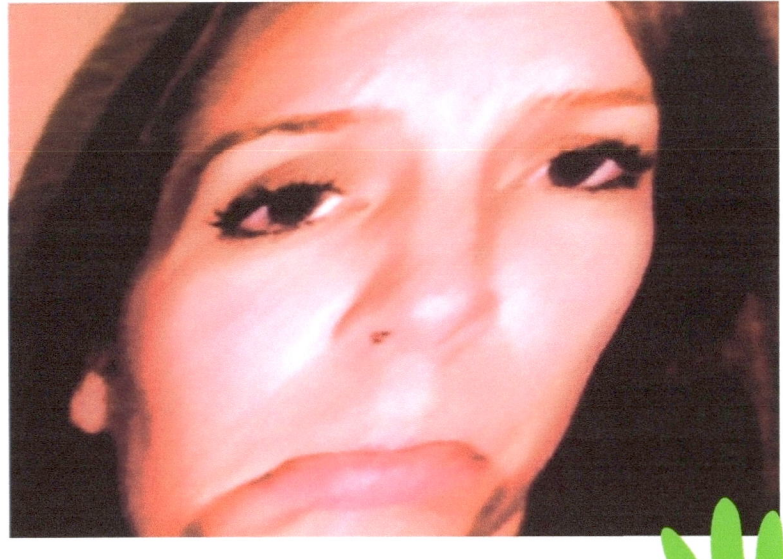

5

But it
hasn't
worked
yet...
so she
needs
help!

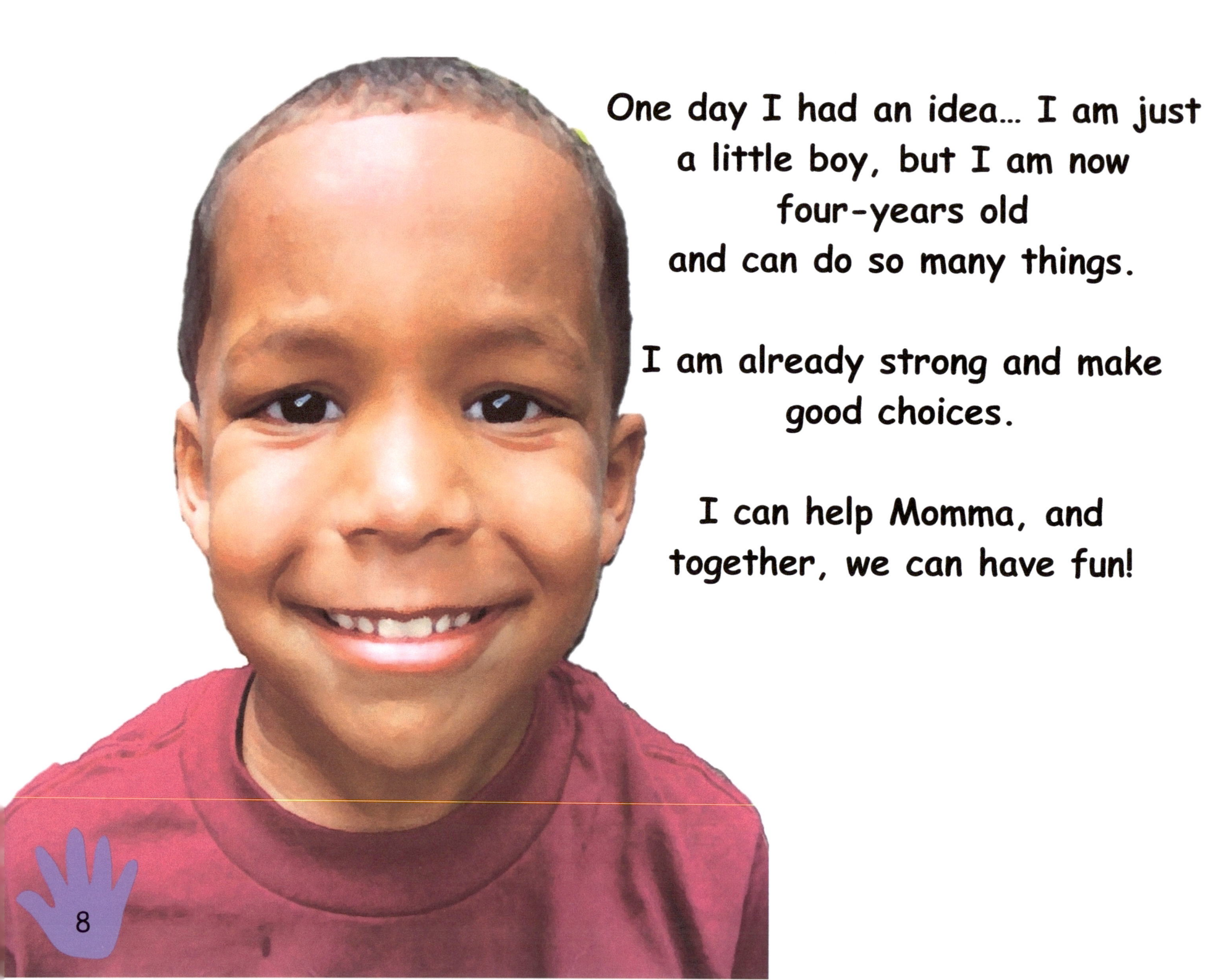

One day I had an idea... I am just a little boy, but I am now four-years old and can do so many things.

I am already strong and make good choices.

I can help Momma, and together, we can have fun!

8

Some things
I love to do!

...Climb up high...

...Paint and
color my
artwork

...Play with friends...

...Play ball...

9

...And pretend

10

I love to play!

I also like to use a lot of toys and other things to play with...

So sometimes...

11

It can get very messy!

I can play and clean up my

messes!

13

Two things I know I have...

My kind heart...

My helpful hands

Our family has

3

Important rules

Be Safe
Be Kind
Be Responsible

I just get started putting things away. It's not easy, but I can do it.

I love it when Momma can help me with these jobs!

16

Washing and taking care of clothes takes a lot of time. Dirty clothes can pile up quick.

I put light clothes into one pile and dark clothes into another.

I take a little rest when I finish.

17

Mine

There is a LOT of laundry for our whole family, but I know how to pick out my own clothes.

When my
clothes
are done,
I put them
in my basket
and take
them to
my room.

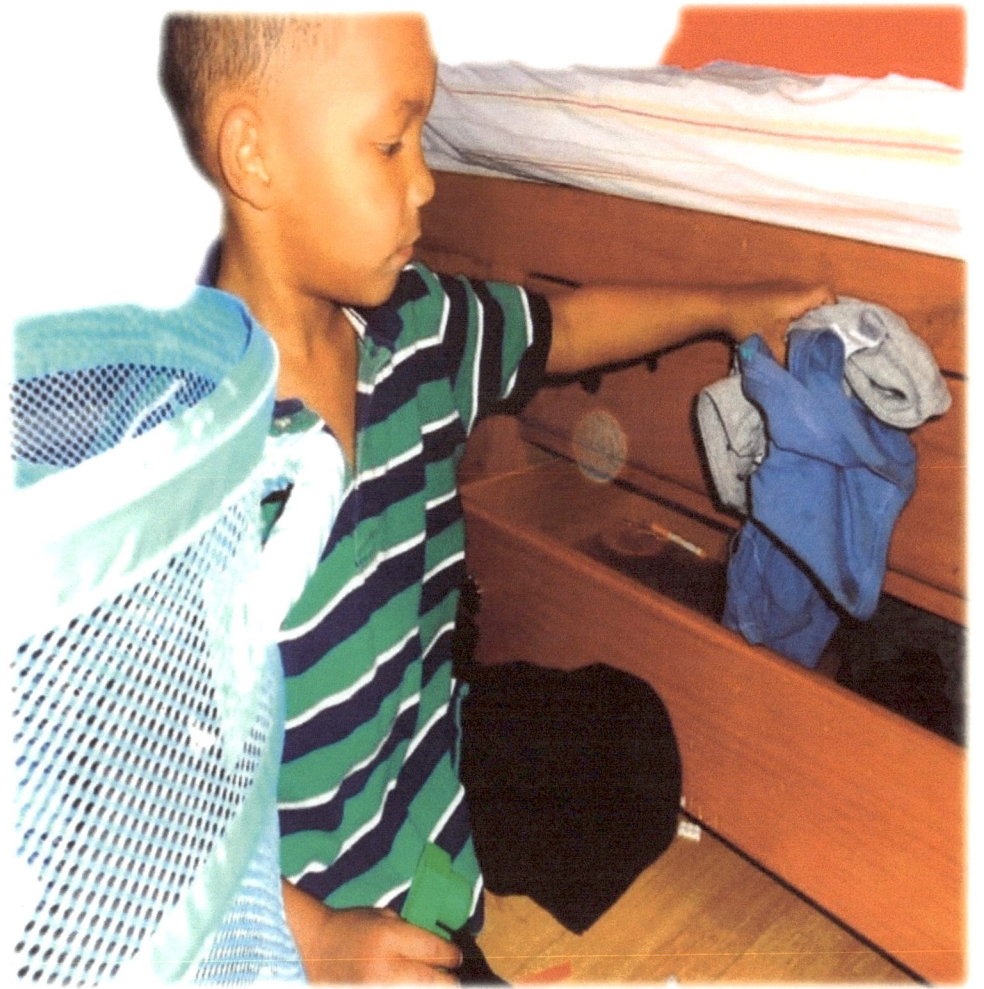

Then I put them away in
my drawer and close it.
I am responsible for my
clothes.

Momma showed me how
to wash windows and get
almost EVERY dirt spot off!

With a spray bottle of water
and a cloth, I can clean off the
table anytime it looks dirty.

Yum! Dinner time-Do I know where the forks and spoons are? Yes! Can I take them out of the drawer, close it, and set the table? Yes, with my magic helpful hands and my blue stool.

I can wash off all the dirty dishes after we eat.

It's fun to help water the plants that make our yard so pretty.

I am strong enough to use our big wheelbarrow and clean up our yard.

My big brother, Jaxon, helps me rake our yard.

I can sweep our porch with the broom!

23

When I see toys scattered around, I clean them up wherever they are.

Sometimes our family takes off our shoes when we sit in the living room. All of our shoes almost fill a room!

I know how to put them back where they belong. It also makes it safer so we don't fall over all those shoes!

When I visit my Grandma's house, Jaxon and I always keep our shoes in the same spot. We are responsible for our own toys and clothes if we go places.

I know how to fill my dog's dish with food, and I do it everyday.

If dog food spills, I pick up the pieces and throw them away. It's so easy! I am responsible and kind to my dog.

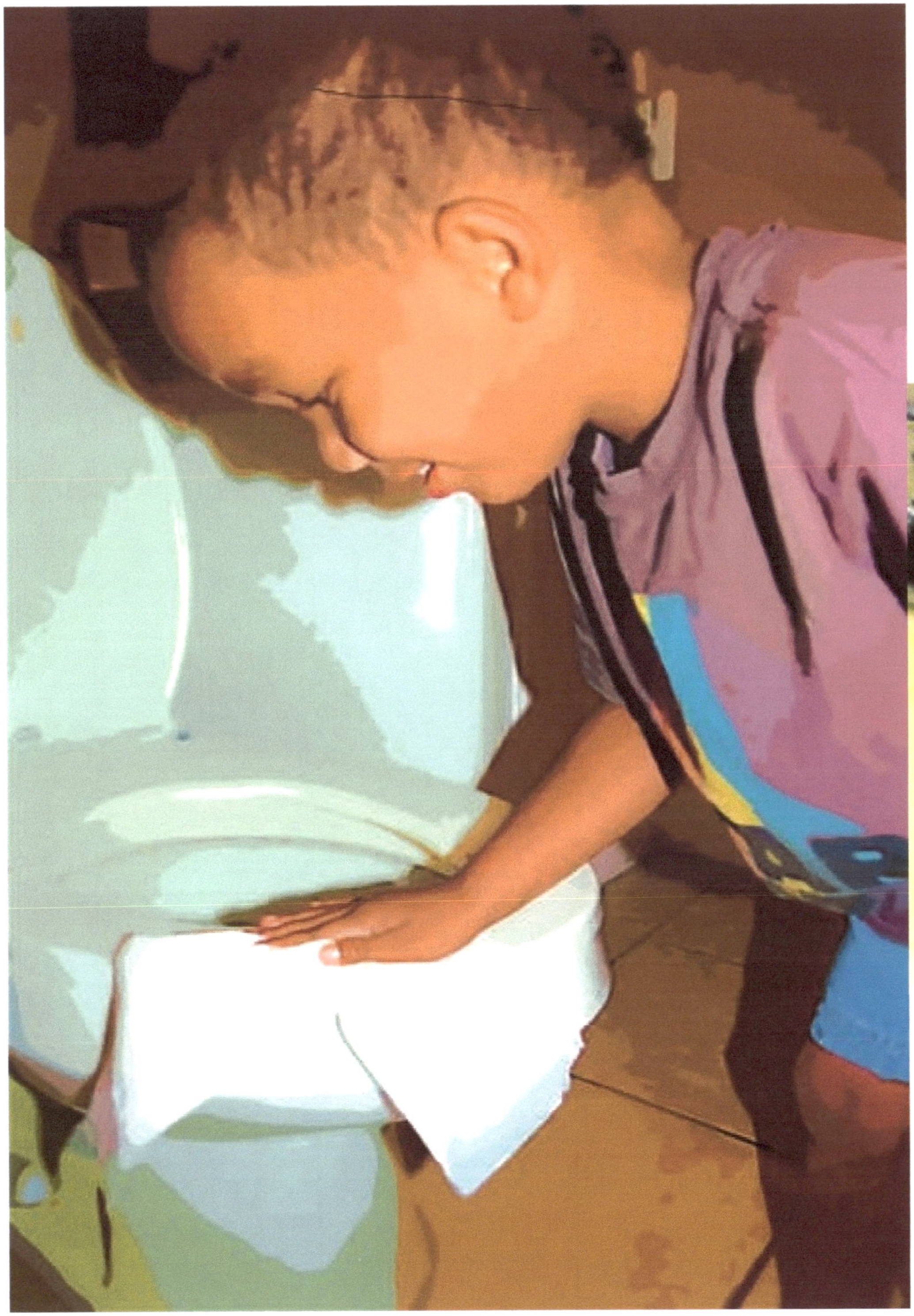

I wipe off areas that look dirty and then wash my hands!

Momma says, "If you sprinkle when you tinkle, please be neat and wipe the seat!"

27

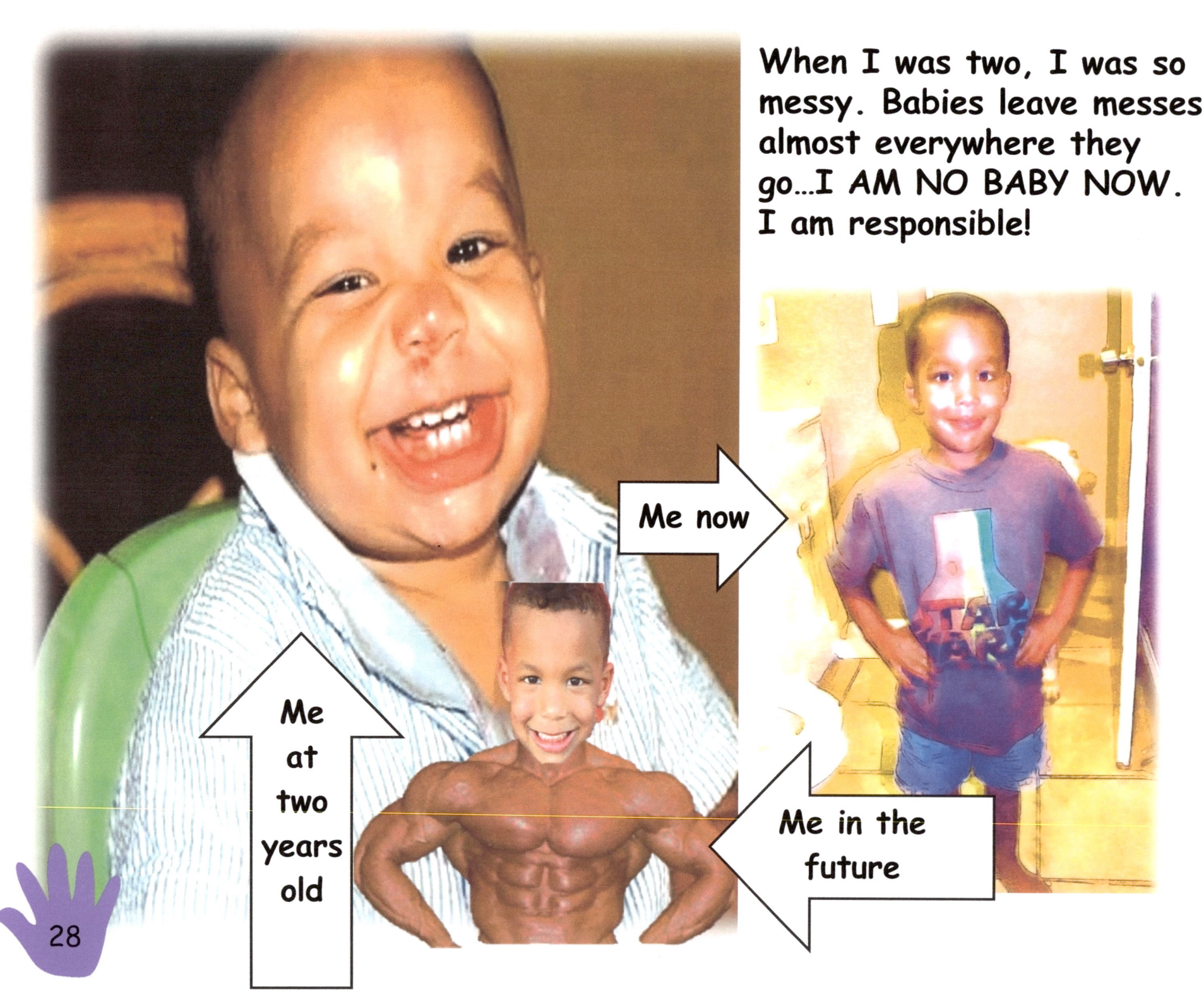

When I was two, I was so messy. Babies leave messes almost everywhere they go...I AM NO BABY NOW. I am responsible!

Me now

Me at two years old

Me in the future

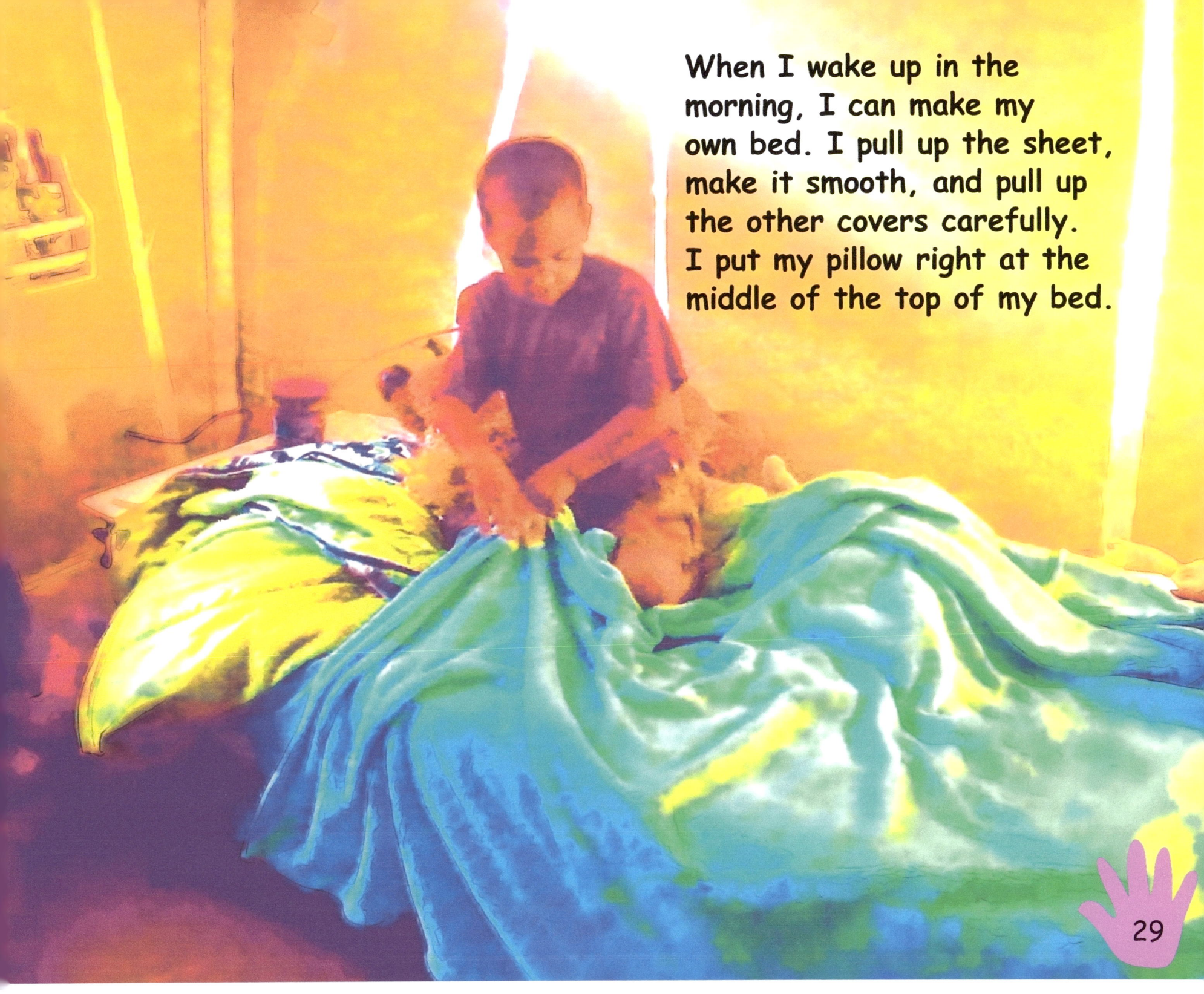

When I wake up in the morning, I can make my own bed. I pull up the sheet, make it smooth, and pull up the other covers carefully. I put my pillow right at the middle of the top of my bed.

29

Now I can fasten my own seat belt to make sure I am safe. All Momma has to do is check it.

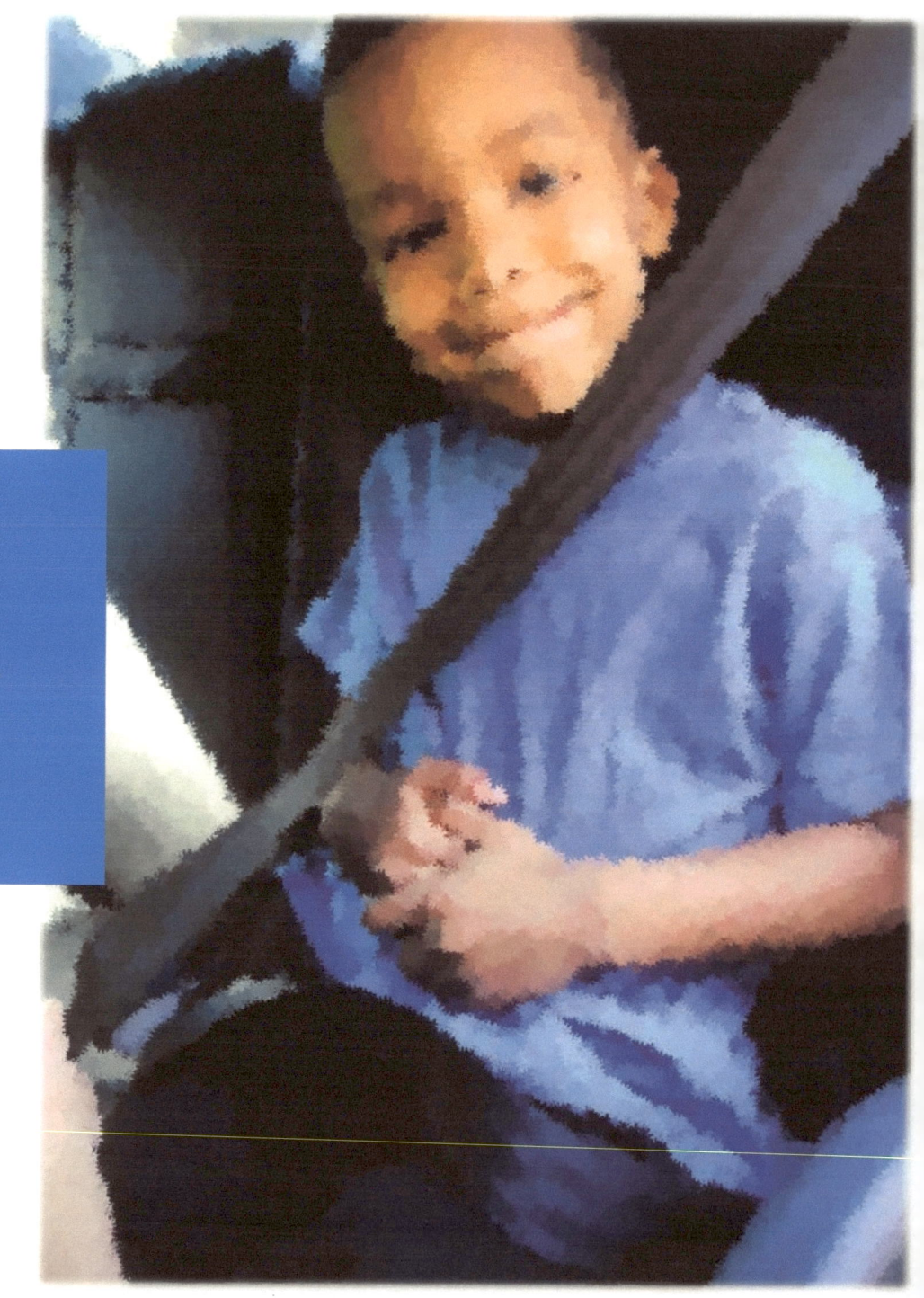

Saul is three, and he sets the table each night.

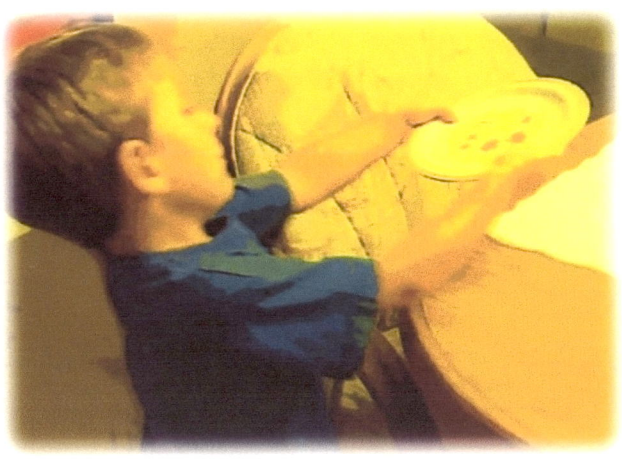

I learn more ways of being helpful by watching other kids.

Maria and Juanita carry a bag to the park for their toys. They don't lose them.

Ali knows how to pick up trash at the park, and he is only two.

31

Getting food for our home is a lot of work!

After I take the bags into the house, I can put the cereal away in the cupboard in the right places.

Sometimes these bags are not easy to lift, but I am strong!

We help Momma cook; stirring, pouring, and measuring is great when we do it together.

33

When we use our power to help each other, we have more time for fun together!

THE END

34

www.ingramcontent.com/pod-product-compliance
Lightning Source LLC
Chambersburg PA
CBHW040813120626

46547CB00004B/540